Let's Count Coins

Putting Data in

I0901576

Spencer Toole

COMPUTER SCIENCE For the REAL World™

Rosen Classroom™

This bank is full of coins!
How can you count coins?

First, put the coins in piles. There are pennies, nickels, dimes, and quarters.

This is a penny.
It is worth 1 cent.

There are 10 pennies.
How many cents are there?
There are 10 cents.

This is a nickel. Each nickel is worth 5 cents.

There are 8 nickels. That makes 40 cents.

There are 5 dimes in all. Dimes are worth 10 cents each. That makes 50 cents.

There are 3 quarters in all.
Quarters are worth 25 cents.
That makes 75 cents.

Look at the coins. Which pile has the most coins? Which pile has the fewest?

What else can you tell from ordering coins? Which pile of coins is worth the most?

Words to Know

dime

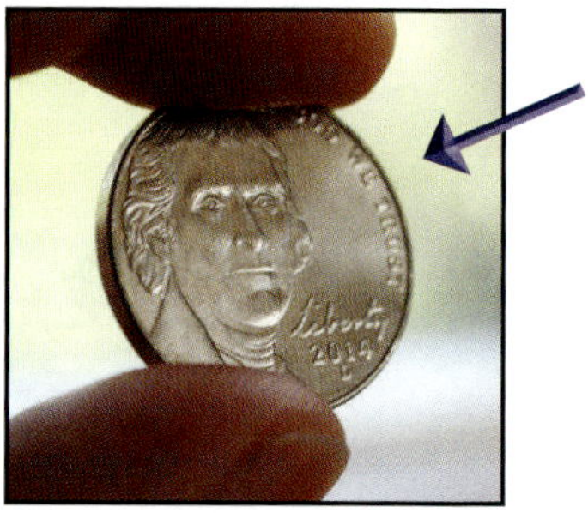

nickel

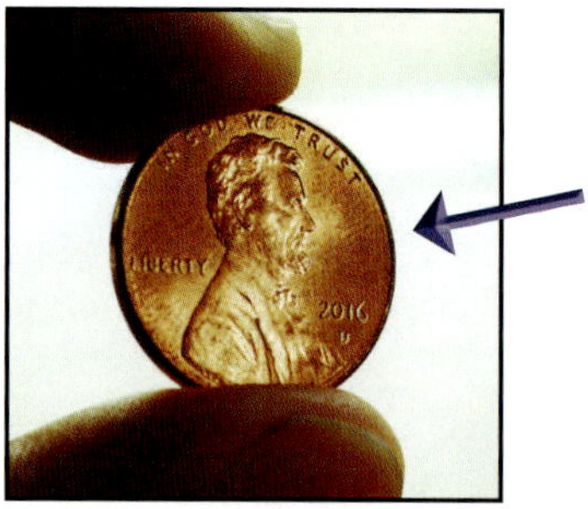

penny

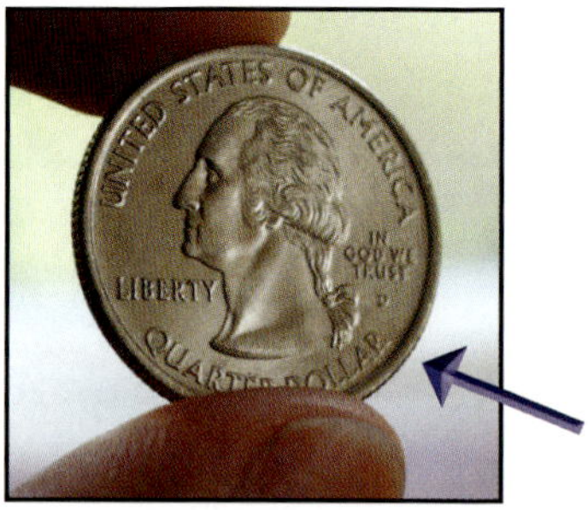

quarter